DAY TRADING

The crash course beginners' guide strategies to trading options and stocks for a living. Psychology and money management for making money and passive income profits

Author Name:

Andrew Steve Hammer

Table of Contents

Introduction

Day trading entails buying and selling of stocks within the same day. It enables you grow your income through making profit from stock price changes that occur during the day. To successfully engage in day trading, it is important to understand how it works.

This trading strategy allows you to maximize on the volume and volatility of stocks to generate income. It presents you with vast opportunities to make money from average amounts of capital. You can make profit both from the downward and upward movement of prices, which is a good thing.

As a day trader, you engage the services of a broker to purchase stock then sell it at a profit. Most of this happens during morning hours when the stock market is still volatile.

This book outlines several important aspects of day trading. It highlights all the requirements for day trading and what you need to do once you start the business, It also informs you of the different strategies you can use in day trading, the common mistakes people make when engaging in the trade as well as the tips you should use to succeed in the trade.

While going through the book, you will learn how to enter and exit trades and how to reduce the risks associated with this short-term trading technique. The book also provides you with guidelines necessary for day trading different financial instruments such as options and futures. If you study it keenly, you will attain your financial goals more quickly as you upgrade your knowledge of the trade. Ideally, this book serves a as a great asset to new day traders as well as those who are experienced in the trade.

Chapter 1: Basics of Day Trading & Qualities of a Day Trader

Before the invention of online trading platforms, people could only engage in stock market trading through brokerage firms, financial institutions, and other trading houses. As more inventions related to the internet were made, it became easy for individual traders to invest in the stock market. One way you can make money on the stock market is through day trading.

Day trading is one technique that can help you gain a lot of income if used properly. However, it becomes a challenge for those who have little information or those who lack the right trading strategies. Sometimes, even the most experienced traders end up losing a fortune because of inadequate knowledge and planning.

Definition

Day trading refers to a technique of stock trading that involves buying and selling of security or assets within a single day. Although day trading takes place in most marketplaces, it is more common in forex and stock trading platforms. For you to succeed in this kind of trade, you must have enough capital. The main goal is to leverage the profit on every slight price movement.

When day trading, you must ensure that each position you open closes by the end of the same day. This means that you cannot hold a position overnight. Instead, you must close the position in the evening and reopen it the next day. It is the opposite of long-term trading where you purchase stock, hold it for some time then sell it off at a profit. That is why day trading is not considered as a form of investment.

Individuals who engage in this kind of trade are known as day traders. As a day trader, you must master how prices move in the marketplace. This is important if you want to make a profit from each short term price movement. A trader can make an unlimited number of trades within a single day. However, beginners can limit themselves to one or a few trades depending on the amount of capital and time available. If a trade does not seem quite profiting at the end of the day, you may decide to let it continue to the next day. However, you will be required to pay some fee to your broker for this to happen.

How long each transaction lasts depends on the trader. Some complete trades in a matter of seconds or minutes while others take several hours. Traders who purchase and sell multiple times within the same day usually end up with high-profit volumes. Some traders prefer selling their stock as soon as a good profit has been realized. Others prefer to wait until the close of the day to end their positions.

Qualities of a Good Day Trader

Day traders who engage in the business as a career always seek to improve their skills each day. They possess in depth knowledge of the market as well as the strategies required to make good cash from the market. So, who is the right person to engage in day trading? Let us look at some of the characteristics one should possess.

1. *Market Experience* – if you happen to engage in day trading without the requisite knowledge of the market, you may lose all your capital. You must be good at reading charts and carrying out technical analysis of the prices and market trends. You must also be able to carry out all the due diligence required to ensure you maximize the profits you realize from the trade.

2. *Adequate capital* – like any other trade, you need sufficient amounts of money to day trade. You must understand that this should be risk capital that you are ready to lose in case the market does not perform in your favor. Preparing yourself this way will save you the emotional torture associated with loss of cash in the trade. You must invest large capitals if you want to make more significant returns.

3. *A good strategy* – several strategies are involved in day trading. You need these strategies to stay ahead of other traders on the market. Before you start trading, you must understand how to apply these strategies in your transactions. When used

correctly, these strategies ensure more consistent returns and fewer losses.

4. *Discipline* – it is essential to be disciplined as a day trader. Without discipline, it becomes difficult to record any successful transactions. Day trading depends on the volatility of stock prices. Traders are often interested in stocks whose price changes a lot in the course of the day. However, if you are not disciplined enough in the way you select your shares, you may end up losing a lot despite the substantial price changes.

This trait is particularly crucial because the stock market has uncountable trading opportunities. You may decide to trade on several industries, products, and assets, but the truth is – not all these opportunities are good for making a profit. If you are disciplined enough, you will spend time analyzing opportunities before investing in them. You will also open and close trades at the right time, and this will ensure that you minimize losses.

5. *Patience* – day trading involves a certain level of waiting. You need to time when to enter the market and when to exit. Getting into the market

blindly always results in a lot of problems. You must be patient enough to get into trades in good time.

Besides being patient, you also need to adapt to the changes taking place in the market. For instance, how a market appears at the beginning of the day is not the same way it will be at midday. You must be able to adjust your strategies to accommodate market changes accordingly.

Most successful day traders always seek to acquire these characteristics as a way of improving their business. Doing this requires a high level of mental as well as financial flexibility. You must be thick-skinned enough to risk your capital and accept any losses that come along. Remember, the main difference between successful and unsuccessful day traders lies in the profits. More profits depict you as a successful trader while less profits display you as one that is on the losing end. However, losing trades should not make you focus less because even professional day traders started by losing.

Chapter 2: Day Trading Tools

For you to carry out day trading successfully there are several tools that you need. Some of these tools are freely available, while others must be purchased. Modern trading is not like the traditional version. This means that you need to get online to access day trading opportunities.

Therefore, the number one tool you need is a laptop or computer with an internet connection. The computer you use must have enough memory for it to process your requests fast enough. If your computer keeps crashing or stalling all the time, you will miss out on some lucrative opportunities. There are trading platforms that need a lot of memory to work, and you must always put this into consideration.

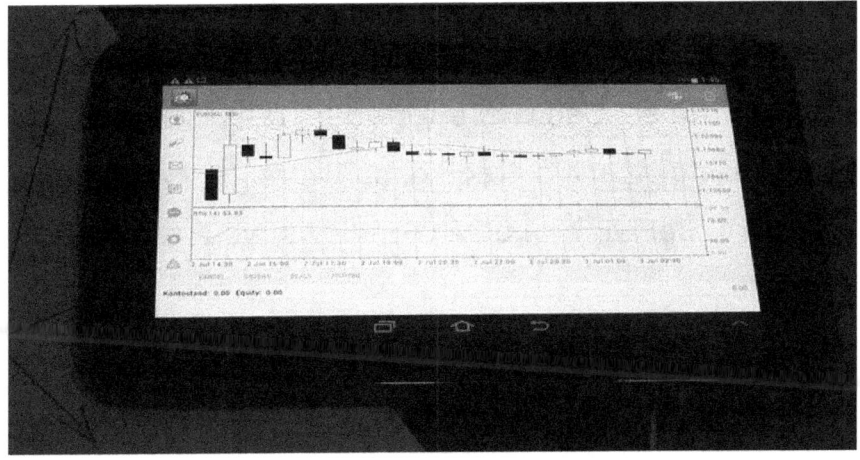

Your internet connection must also be fast enough. This will ensure that your trading platform loads in real-time. Ensure that you get an internet speed that processes data instantaneously to avoid experiencing any data lag. Due to some outages that occur with most internet providers, you may also need to invest in a backup internet device such as a smartphone hotspot or modem. Other essential tools and services that you need include:

Brokerage

To succeed in day trading, you need the services of a brokerage firm. The work of the firm is to conduct your trades. Some brokers are experienced in day trading than others. You must ensure that you get the right day trading broker who can help you make more profit from your transactions. Since day trading entails several trades per day, you need a broker that offers lower commission rates. You also need one that provides the best software for your transactions. If you prefer using specific trading software for your deals, then look for a broker that allows you to use this software.

Real-time Market Information

Market news and data are essential when it comes to day trading. They provide you with the latest updates on current and anticipated price changes on the market. This information allows you to customize your strategies accordingly. Professional day traders always spend a lot of money seeking this kind of information on news platforms, in online forums or through any other reliable channels.

Financial data is often generated from price movements of specific stocks and commodities. Most brokers have this information. However, you will need to specify the kind of data you need for your trades. The type of data to get depends on the type of stocks you wish to trade.

Monitors

Most computers have a capability that enables them to connect to more than one monitor. Due to the nature of the day trading business, you need to track market trends, study indicators, follow financial news items, and monitor price performance at the same time. For this to be possible, you need to have more than one processor so that the above tasks can run concurrently.

Classes

Although you can engage in day trading without attending any school, you must get trained on some of the strategies you need to succeed in the business. For instance, you may decide to enroll for an online course to acquire the necessary knowledge in the business. You may have all the essential tools in your possession, but if you do not have the right experience, all your efforts may go to waste.

Day Trading Pricing Charts

Charts are used by traders to monitor price changes. These changes determine when to enter or exit a trading position. There are several charts used in day trading. Although these charts differ in terms of functionality and layout, they typically offer the same information to day traders.

Some of the most common day trading charts includes:

1. Line charts
2. Bar charts
3. Candlestick charts

For each of the above charts, you must understand how they work as well as the advantages/ disadvantages involved.

Line Charts

These are very popular in all kinds of stock trading. They do not give the opening price, just the closing price. You are expected to specify the trading period for the chart to display the closing price for that period. The chart creates a line that connects closing prices for different periods using a line.

Most day traders use this chart to establish how the price of a security has performed over different periods. However, you cannot rely on this chart as the only information provider when it comes to making some critical trading decisions. This is because the chart only gives you the closing price. This means that you may not be able to establish other vital factors that have contributed to the current changes in the price.

Bar Charts

These are lines used to indicate price ranges for a particular stock over time. Bar charts comprise vertical and horizontal lines. The horizontal lines often represent the opening and closing costs. When the closing price is higher than the opening price, the horizontal line is always black. When the opening price is higher, the line becomes red.

Bar charts offer more information than line charts. They indicate opening prices, highest and lowest prices as well as the closing prices. They are always easy to read and interpret. Each bar represents rice information. The vertical lines indicate the highest and lowest prices attained by a particular stock. The opening price of a stock is always shown using a small horizontal line on the left of each vertical line. The closing price is a small horizontal line on the right.

Interpreting bar charts is not as easy as interpreting line charts. When the vertical lines are long, it shows that there is a significant difference between the highest price attained by a security and the lowest price. Large vertical lines, therefore, indicate that the commodity is highly volatile while small lines indicate slight price changes. When the closing price is far much higher than the opening price, it means that the buyers were more during the stated period. This indicates likelihood for more purchases in the future. If the closing price is slightly higher than the purchase price, then very little purchasing took place during the period. Bar chart information is always differentiated using color codes. You must, therefore, understand what each color means as this will help you to know whether the price is going up or down.

Advantages of bar charts

- They display a lot of data in a visual format

- They summarize large amounts of data

- They help you to estimate important price information in advance

- They indicate each data category as a different color

- Exhibit high accuracy

- Easy to understand

Disadvantages

- They need adequate interpretation

- Wrong interpretation can lead to false information

- Do not explain changes in the price patterns

Tick charts

Tick charts are not common in day trading. However, some traders use these charts for various purposes. Each bar on the chart represents numerous transactions. For instance, a 415 chart generates a bar for a group of 415 trade positions. One great advantage of tick charts is that they enable traders to enter and exit multiple positions quickly. This is what makes the charts ideal for day traders who transact volumes of stock each day.

These charts work by completing several trades before displaying a new bar. Unlike other charts, these charts work depending on the activity of each transaction, not on time. You can use them if you need to make faster decisions in your trade. Another advantage of tick charts is that you can customize each chart to suit your trading needs. You can apply the chart on diverse transaction sizes. The larger the size, the higher the potential of making a profit from the trade.

When used in day trading, tick hart works alongside the following three indicators:

- *RSI indicators* – these are used when trading highly volatile securities. They help you establish when a particular security is oversold or overbought since these are the periods when stock prices change significantly.

- *Momentum* – day traders use this together with tick charts to show how active the stock price is and whether the activity is genuine or fake. If the price rises significantly, yet the momentum is the same, this indicates a warning sign. Stocks with positive momentum are ideal for long trades. You should avoid these if you wish to close your positions within a day.

- *Volume indicators* – these are used to confirm the correct entry and exit points for each trade. Large trading positions are often indicated using larger volume bars while low positions with little volatility are displayed using small volume bars.

Candlestick Charts

Candlestick charts are used on almost every trading platform. These charts carry a lot of information about the stock market and stock prices. They help you to get information about the opening, closing, highest, and lowest stock prices on the market. The opening price is always indicated as the first bar on the left of the chart, and the closing price is on the far right of the chart. Besides these prices, the candlestick chart also contains the body and wick. These are the features that differentiate the candlestick for other day trading charts.

One great advantage of candlestick charts entails the use of different visual aspects when indicating the closing, opening, highest, and lowest stock prices. These charts compute stock prices across different time frames. Each chart consists of three segments:

- The upper shadow

- The body

- The lower shadow

The body of the chart is often red or green in color. Each candlestick is an illustration of time. The data in the candlestick represents the number of trades completed within the specified time. For instance, a 10-minute candlestick indicates 10 minutes of trading. Each candlestick has four points, and each point represents a price. The high point represents the highest stock price while low stands for the lowest price of a stock. When the closing price is lower than the opening price, the body of the candlestick will be red in color. When the closing price is higher, the body will be colored green.

There are several types of candlesticks that you can use in day trading. One is the Heikin-Ashi chart that helps you to filter any unwanted information from the chart data, ending up with a more accurate indication of the market trend. Novice day traders commonly use this chart because of how clear it displays information.

The Renko chart only displays the changes in time. It does not give you any volume or time information. When the price exceeds the highest or lowest points reached before, the chart displays it as a new brick. The brick is white when the price is going up and black when the price is declining.

Lastly, the Kagi chart is used when you want to follow the direction of the market quickly. When the price goes higher than previous prices, the chart displays a thick line. When the price starts to decline, the line reduces in thickness.

Each of the above charts works using a time frame which is represented using the X-axis. This time frame always indicates the volume of information represented by the chart. Time frames can be in the form of standard time or in the form of the number of trades completed within a specified period as well as the price range.

Charting Software

Each of the above charts is created and viewed using specific software. This can be found in a brokerage firm, although you may also purchase this online depending on the type you want to use.

The software helps you identify the right opportunities by indicating when and how you should start and close positions. They always display the necessary patterns required to estimate future changes in stock prices. Using stock patterns, you can also establish continuations as well as reversals in the stock prices.

Chart software is available in many forms. You may find those that are in the form of mobile apps or others that are web-based. Getting the right software enables you to generate correct charts. This explains why you also need to incorporate technical analysis in your trades.

Most day trading chart tools are available free of charge. Some have a forum where you can learn from experienced traders as you use them. They also come with demo accounts that enable you to master day trading techniques before investing your capital in the business.

How to Choose Day Trading Charts

Before selecting any charts for your day trading engagements, you must consider a number of factors. These include:

1. *Responsiveness* - This refers to how quickly the chart can display information about the changing market features. This is the first and most important factor you should always check out for. Any delay in

the way a chart displays data means that you will not receive vital information in real-time. You may end up acting on old information to make your decisions, and this can lead to significant losses on your part. Most charts may freeze or crash when your computer runs out of memory. This explains why you need a fast processing machine for your day trading business. You want to ensure that the whole process remains as efficient as possible. When testing a chart for responsiveness, wait for a time when the stock market is busy. For instance, you may try using the chart during a critical financial announcement or news session. If the chart freezes at this point, then you will understand that it is not the best for your needs.

2. *Cost* – every trader wants to invest in tools that cost less to acquire and maintain. Years back, trading charts used to cost a fortune. This limited the number of traders that could engage in day trading. For instance, traders could buy market data from stock exchanges, and this would also cost a lot of money. Nowadays, all information required for any kind of trading is cheaply available. This means that charts should also not cost as much. There are several alternatives available on the market today

for you to select from. As you do this, always have the price in mind.

3. *Stability* – a good chart is one that remains online and up to date all the time. For you to succeed as a day trader, you must remain on the market most of the time. If your chart keeps disconnecting from the stock market or fails to display market information on time, then it will make you incur more losses. You must, therefore, ensure that you remain connected to the market continuously. If you experience instability as a result of the chart software you are using, feel free to change it. If the instability is resulting from a poor internet connection, you may need to replace it too.

4. *Type of Indicators* – if you have ever engaged in day trading before then you understand the importance of technical indicators. Having the right indicators plays a vital role in ensuring you predict the right price movements in the future. Indicators help you to save a lot of capital. They prevent you from making important investment and financial mistakes that may lead to losing your capital. You may create your own indicators, or you may get charting software that has in-built indicators. If you decide to

use your own indicators, you must ensure that the charting tools you purchase can be used together with these indicators. If not, you might need to stick to those indicators supplied together with your charting software.

5. *Compatibility with your computer* – before settling for any charts, check whether it will work well with your current computer resources. This is an important factor as it will determine whether you will continue to use your old machine, or if you will have to purchase a new one. Some charts require a lot of RAM space. If your computer does not have this capability, you will end up adding more RAM. This translates to more yet unnecessary costs. When you are looking around for a chart, ensure that you check how much resources the charts will need. Most chart packages have an indication of the minimum requirements you need for the charts to work well. If this is not clearly stated, make sure you ask your provider about it so that you do not make a blind purchase.

6. *User-friendly* - a good chart should be easy to use, read, and interpret. A complicated chart will only make your trading days difficult. Get a chart that

simplifies the work of interpreting data. Take your time and research on the available options then choose the best in terms of simplicity and layout. You may consider getting recommendations from other traders, although this does not necessarily mean that the said chart will work for you. Having a complicated chart can make you lose your confidence. You must, therefore, avoid it if you want to have a smooth trading experience

7. *End-user support* – once in a while, your chart software may experience a problem that needs technical assistance. As you continue using the software, questions may arise that need the attention of an expert. If the provider is not available to assist or respond to your questions, you may get stuck using the package. Before making a purchase, ensure that you find out the kind of technical support you will receive and how this will be done. Is it via live chat, email, or telephone contact? You can also go through some customer reviews just to understand if the service provider has a history of supporting its clients on technical matters. In case you need a highly responsive system, you may need to avoid those platforms that use the support ticket criteria. Companies that use

this criterion to solve customer problems always take a long time to respond to even the most critical issues.

Charts play an essential role, and you can use timed as well as ticked charts for successful day trading. Always remember that different tools are designed for different kinds of trades. You must understand the kind of tools you need as a day trader so that you do not struggle on the market.

Chapter 3: Understanding Futures & Day Trading Orders

Futures are agreements created to either purchase or sell a particular security at a later date and at specific prices. Futures are normally traded on an exchange similar to stocks and options. An individual commits to purchasing a certain amount of securities or assets, and the seller undertakes to deliver the same at a future date. People who engage in trading futures include investors, companies as well as speculators.

Just like options, futures represent derivatives of an underlying stock. This means that the price of a futures contract changes depending on changes in the underlying instrument. The process of day trading futures is different from trading stocks because when trading futures, you do not get to own the shares associated with the lying instrument.

There are several reasons why people engage in day trading using futures. Some of these include:

- *Low prices* – when day trading stocks, the capital requirements are too high. However, you do not need a lot of capital to trade in futures. You can start trading with as low as $5000, or less depending on the trading platform.

- *Price changes with the underlying security* – the amount of profit you make from day trading futures is determined by the price changes in the underlying security. This implies that you can use technical analysis strategies to leverage the income you receive from trading futures.

- *No short-selling restrictions* – short-term traders often depend on each trade to realize some good profits. When trading futures, there are no restrictions on both long and short trading positions. This means that you can apply market analysis information on all kinds of futures. This is not the case with stock day trading since you must have stock in place before selling it at a profit. This restriction makes it impossible for you to short-sell when trading stocks.

To start day trading futures, you need a few tools and resources similar to those required when selling stocks. There are minimum capital regulations to be met, and you must also work through a broker. Once you identify a broker, you will need to select the kind of futures contract you wish to trade. When doing this, there are several factors that you must consider including the volume of trade and previous price movement of the futures contract, among others.

There are several risks involved in day trading futures as well. Most traders always borrow capital to invest in the futures market because of the substantial profit margins involved. Small price changes still result in exponentially significant returns. However, trading in futures using borrowed money always results in high risk. If the market direction does not assume the expected direction, you will end up losing the borrowed money. Futures possess a high leverage potential that traders take advantage of. This leverage presents a high-profit potential, but also creates a platform for more significant loss.

Day Trading Orders

Stock trading involves a lot more than selling and buying of assets and securities. There are several orders used in each technique of trading. Each order is created to fulfill a particular task on the market. Let us look at some of the orders you can employ in day trading and how you can use them.

- *Market Order is* one of the easiest orders to raise. It can be divided into two – market orders for buying and market orders for selling. This order provides you information about the market price. For instance, if you create a market order to purchase a particular asset or derivative. You will be able to see a list of all the sellers on the market plus the price of their securities. If you raise an order to sell, you will gain access to a list of available buyers together with their bid prices. Day traders use market orders to enter or exit trades faster, especially when the prices are changing drastically.

The disadvantage of market orders, though, is that you can never tell the exact opening or closing price of a transaction. The prices always depend on the volume of the stock you decide to trade in.

- *Buy stop order* is placed by day traders seeking to purchase stocks at a price that is higher than the current price. The order is filled when the price goes above the indicated stop price. The order is mostly used to restrict losses incurred on a short trade position when the market prices start moving in an unfavorable direction.

- *Sell stop order* is utilized when the price drops below the current stock price. When you raise this order, it can only be filled when the stop price is higher or the same as the current stock price. Day traders use this kind of order to exit long trades that have assumed a losing direction.

- *Buy limit order* is placed when the day trader wishes to purchase at a cost that is lower than the current stock price. This gives you an opportunity to control the amount of cash you pay for a particular purchase position. When you create a buy limit order, you can only buy the stock at the current price or lower, not higher. One disadvantage of this kind of order is that you are never sure if it will be filled. If the amount of stock keeps going higher than the current price, then you will not succeed in purchasing any stock.

- *Sell limit order* is the opposite of the buy limit order. When you raise this order, you are indicating a willingness to sell a security or asset at a price that is higher than the current stock price. Like the buy limit order, you can only fill this order if the price rises above the current price. The aim of using this order is to make you generate profit from any long trades that you engage in.

- *Buy stop limit order* works the same way as the buy stop order, only that is works differently from the market order. This order gets completed when the price of the stock reaches the buy stop limit amount or less. It prevents you from paying more than the anticipated amount for each trade thus reducing the number of losses you may incur

- *Sell stop limit order* - sell stop limit order also plays the same role as the sell stop order but does not mimic the market order. When you place this kind of order, it only gets filled when the stock price attains an amount that is equal or more than the stop limit price. Setting the wrong order for your day trading activities can cause you to end into problems. The more you practice how to use the orders, the more you will understand how and when to apply them.

What Day Traders Do Every day

A typical day in the life of the day trader is often filled with lots of exciting activities. What the trader spends time doing during the day determines the amount of profit he makes at the end of the day. Some of the days are always smooth and less busy while others involve a lot of activities.

Traders rise early enough to study the market as they prepare for the day. Depending on one's location, morning hours may present some excellent trading opportunities or some not so good ones. Day traders always take advantage of this period because the prices are the most liquid, and the most volatile. Here are some of the primary stages a day trader goes through each day

1. *Preparing for the day*

Day traders always take time to prepare for the day as a way of ensuring that things go as planned during the entire day. Some ensure that they get up at least an hour before the trading session begins. This is in order to:

- Go through the necessary strategies for the day and resolve any issues faced the previous day

- Create a trading plan for the day or revise existing plans accordingly

- Adjust account balances accordingly and determine how much they are ready to risk losing that day

- Check any changes in price and financial news that can affect market direction

- Analyze the trading platform to ensure it's still working well

2. *Trading Session*

Day traders always make transactions the first few hours after the market opens. Depending on how active the market is, some opt to trade for more extended periods, until most of the stocks become less volatile.

Although beginners in the trade always think that they have to spend a lot of time online to make a profit, this is not the case. Professional day traders only visit the trading platforms to enter or exit positions and set the necessary orders for the day. Once some orders are filled, trades associated with such orders always close automatically. This means that you do not need to spend all your time on day trading platforms to make a profit.

3. *Review*

Takes place at the end of the trading day. For some, the day can end as early as 11:00 am while for others; it may end as late as 6:00 pm. At this point, the trader goes through the day's business and notes down every activity and results of each trade. This is where the trader also calculates the profits or losses incurred and notes down what needs to be done to improve future trading experiences. A basic review always consists of the number of hours spent on the trading platform and the number of positions completed successfully. It also consists of the number of successful or unsuccessful trades as well as the net profit or loss.

Without the right plan and strategy, day trading becomes a less exciting venture. However, traders who have mastered the necessary moves on the market always enjoy every bit of the business. The secret to becoming better at the trade lies in doing a lot of practice.

Trading Goals for Overcoming Constraints

Trading goals are different from ordinary goals. The main purpose for each trader is always to make a profit from each trade. However, day trading goals go beyond basic selling and buying of stocks at a profit. Several attributes define achievable day trading goals:

- *They focus on the trading process and not the benefits.* You probably know that the main focus of creating goals is making them specific and measurable. In day trading, you must ensure that the goals you make do not focus on the amount of money you wish to build over time. You should instead concentrate on the efforts you need to put in the process you use. When the process is perfect, the results will automatically be positive

- *They are defense-minded.* If you set goals that are not defense-minded, you will end up pursuing trading opportunities only for the sake of financial gain. However, your goals should seek to protect your capital. Doing this will keep you into business even when you are not making any profit. You can do this by setting limit orders for each trading period. Also, you can outline a risk tolerance plan that indicates the amount you are willing to lose in every trade. With these figures in place, you can always customize your strategies and trading techniques to ensure that you do not exceed these limits.

- *They are progressive.* Sound goals allow you to get into the day trading business gradually. They ensure that you do not skip any step of the trading process and that you acquire the necessary training before jumping into the trade. You can do this by ensuring that you do not risk more than you are willing to lose. And that you do not depend on market indicators to make trading decisions all the time.

Setting clear, realistic goals is a must for every day trader. However, you must remember that your goals must never be profit-oriented. This is one grave mistake that most traders make. The right goals will always prevent you from over-risking your capital and overtrading.

Day Trading and Emotions

Day trading involves making quick decisions. This explains why you must always have your emotions under control. If you fail to control them, you may lose any profits and capital accumulated over time in a single trade gone wrong.

When most traders lose part of their capital to some trades, they tend to get frustrated and fearful. This causes them to overleverage the little money remaining. As a result, they end up blowing their account in one or a few risky trades. Day trading is not like other long-term trading strategies where you can quickly determine the direction of market prices. That is why you need to stick to your initial plan and strategy.

One of the attributes that make day traders remain in business is discipline. The strategy demands a lot of concentration and focus. You must, therefore, seek to understand how best to control your emotions when trading. Let us look at some of the things you need to do to avoid emotional trading:

- *Avoid less volatile trading seasons.* Most day traders prefer trading during sessions of high volatility. This sometimes leads to congestion in the marketplace, and if you do not have the right skills and strategies, you may end up frustrated. If the market gets flooded and the prices seem stagnant, avoid entering any positions as this can result in tremendous losses.

- *Exit the market after a few wins.* Once you make three or more consecutive wins, stop trading until another time. This also applies to losing. When you win consecutively, you may start feeling that you are a super trader. In such excitement, you can end up entering the wrong trades, thus losing all your profits. Most people revenge trade as a way of recovering what they have already lost. This results in more losses. Therefore, you should exit the market for a few minutes or hours when you consistently win or lose.

- *Take a break between trades.* Given the rapid changes in market prices when day trading, it is easy for you to get drowned into the trade and forget about your emotions. You must take a break from the trading platform after each trade. This will give you time to reflect on the next move you need to make and give you better control of your emotions.

- *Don't focus on the outcome.* To keep your emotions in check, avoid checking your losses and profits when trading. If you do this, you will definitely experience a surge of emotions that may be difficult to control. Always stick to the rules of trade as you hope to gain some profit at the end of the day.

As you do the above, you must bear in mind that controlling your emotions needs a lot of patience and perseverance. You must keep improving on your emotional stability for the long term success of your business. With time, you will realize that you do not need to concentrate on managing any emotions. You would have rained your brain to respond to the various emotional triggers.

Factors to Consider When Starting Day Trading

To succeed in day trading, there are some few factors you need to put into consideration. Here are some of them.

1. The kind of security to trade. You cannot trade every commodity on the market. You must concentrate on specific products when day trading. When selecting a broker to work with, you will be expected to list the kind of instruments you want to trade in. Most day traders only engage in stock trading. However, there are several other instruments that you can

focus on, such as derivatives, options, and futures.

2. Chose the right broker. Once you identify the kind of instrument to trade, it is also essential that you get the right broker for the instrument. Brokers are often interested in working with day traders because of the high commissions involved. You must be careful that you do not get one that doesn't have experience in this kind of trade. Check out for things like the commissions and margin rates charged to ensure that you remain with some good profits at the end of the day. Also, ensure that the broker offers the best research and trading tools.

3. Set trading sessions. Although day trading does not require that you stick to a particular routine, you can identify specific times that work for you and stick to trading during these times. Most day traders enter the market during morning hours, or a few hours before the day ends. You can choose a time that suits your schedule.

4. Determine how much you can risk in the trade. This will ensure that you do not end up frustrated in case you lose part of your capital. It is always

advisable that you risk 2% or less of your capital for each trade. You must set this time ahead of every trade to ensure that you do not exceed it. You also need to add any interest charges to this amount since most brokers charge a reasonable amount as interest.

Day Trading Stocks and the Strategies Involved

As stated earlier in this chapter, most day traders concentrate on trading stocks more than other financial instruments. Although stocks are considered as great investments for long-term traders, day traders can take advantage of the changes in stock prices to make some profit out of it. Multiple strategies are available for use by day traders who deal with stocks. One of these is scalping which focuses on generating several small profits from the small price changes that occur in the stock market. This strategy focuses on the number of trades, not the quality of trade. Another strategy is the use of moving average crossovers which allows you to make a purchase when a fast-moving average crosses over a slow-moving one.

Chapter 4: Day Trading Pros and Cons

Day trading has become quite popular among online traders in the recent past. With increased advancement in the stock trading industry, day trading has been identified as one of the profitable opportunities that you can engage in. Of course, the main reason why people choose a trading strategy over the other is the potentiality of the approach generating some good income. However, day trading has several better advantages over other trading strategies by far. These advantages are listed below.

Easy to learn – it is easy to learn and start day trading. In case you begin trading using penny stocks, you do not require a license or training to get started. All you need is an internet connection, a functional laptop, and some little capital. However, this becomes a drawback if you start trading without the necessary information. With proper preparation, you can get started without needing any assistance from other traders.

Better control of your capital - This is one of the most exciting aspects of day trading. You are always the determinant factor for your success. You control how your capital gets utilized and how you use the profits realized from the trade. The kind of strategies and plans you come up with determine how much you get at the end of each day. If you do not spend time seeking to understand how the strategy works, you may end up getting frustrated with the business. You are also responsible for determining your schedules. This means that you can do day trading at a time that is convenient for you so long as the market is still open for trading.

Succeeding is easy - One other advantage of day trading is that it has an explicit guarantee of success. This is because stock prices always keep fluctuating every day, meaning that there is always an opportunity to make money out of the business. So long as you are determined to make the right moves on the market, you can be sure of making some profit at the end of the day. Most of the required research is already done by the experts. All you need to do is apply the right types of orders and strategies at the right time.

Availability of Resources – several years ago, traders could pay financial institutions a lot of cash to gain access to market data and other trading resources. With the availability of the internet today, it is very easy to find free, educative resources about day trading online. There are tutorials, workshops, webinars, and free online courses that you can enroll in to gain more understanding of the strategy.

Quick profits - When compared to other trading strategies, day trading offers you a quick turnaround in terms of profit. You do not have to wait for extended periods to gain access to your money since it is made available to you at the end of each trading day. Although there are several risks involved in the trade, the reward potential is too significant to be realized. If you are seeking to make large profits within a short time, you may attempt day trading.

Overnight risks do not exist - In day trading; you close every trade position at the end of the trading day. This ensures that you do not risk your capital by holding onto stocks overnight. Markets change a lot during the night. Holding onto positions the entire night always results in an increased risk of losing your income. As you close the business at the end of each day, you are always sure that you will start afresh the following day without having to incur any more losses.

You can make profit from bad markets - Through the use of short selling and other favorable strategies, day traders can easily make some income from markets whose prices are on the decline. This is one of the most significant pros in day trading.

The use of technical analysis - Traders often uses fundamental and technical analysis to interpret financial market information. Long-term trading strategies always concentrate on using fundamental analysis to determine market prices. Day traders, on the other hand, can utilize technical analysis to determine what is happening on the market at the current moment. Doing this ensures that the traders understand the right time to enter or close positions as a way of making a profit from the business.

Flexible - When it comes to day trading, you are the sole person to determine the kind of markets you trade in and the types of stock you wish to trade. Each trading market has its advantages and disadvantages. Day trading allows you to scan the markets as a way of identifying the best depending on your risk profile, working hours, and trading plan. You can trade any time so long as the markets are open.

Lower commissions - Because you will be working with a broker, it is easy to get a broker that offers extremely low rates. This is a great plus for you if you intend to day trade on a long-term basis. With small commissions, you can easily pocket a good amount of profit since only a little percentage will go to the broker as interest rates.

Provides instant gratification - Day trading gives you the opportunity to make instant profits as soon as you start trading. Once you get onto the trading platform, you start selling or buying immediately.

Besides the numerous advantages of day trading, there are a few risks involved in the business that you also need to be aware of. They are as follows:

- *Information overload.* There is a wide variety of resources online today related to day trading. Most of this information is not accurate and can lead you to losing your capital. It is essential therefore, that you look for information from credible sources, and that you do not get too much of it as this may confuse you. For instance, some sites give traders the impression that day trading guarantees 100 percent profit, yet this is not true. If you come across such hype and you believe it, you may raise your expectations too high. This can cause you to invest your entire fortune in a deal you are not sure to win.

- *Time-consuming.* Day trading needs a lot of time since you must first study the market trends before placing your trades. It becomes difficult if you are doing the business alongside a regular job or other physical businesses. Your work schedule may hinder you from getting the best opportunities.

- May also need to trade outside regular working hours to be able to make a good profit from it. The trade becomes more complicated if you are following more than one market. You may end up overworking yourself, or overspending on a broker that is willing to carry out the trades on your behalf.

- *Too many risks involved.* Although day trading has a high potential for profit, it is too risky if you invest money that you are not willing to lose. It even becomes riskier if you engage in the trade using borrowed capital. Once you miss it, you are left with huge debts to settle.

- *Involves a lot of emotions.* When compared with other types of trading, day trading is more engaging in terms of emotions. Each time you make huge profits or losses, you may get too excited or too anxious, and this can lead to overtrading.

- *Requires accurate timing*. If you take too long to make decisions, then day trading may not work for you. The strategy requires that you make commitments too fast. To do this, you must have the right knowledge and tools for analyzing stock prices and market trends. You must also be confident of each move that you make since this must be done at adequate speeds for you to maximize on the available opportunities.

- *May get boring*. When the stock prices are highly volatile, you may be required to make quick decisions on which positions to buy or sell. However, once you have entered or closed positions, you will have nothing more to do except watch the market for more opportunities. The market may keep moving randomly for a long time as well without providing a chance for you to trade. This results in a waste of time on your part. You will need to monitor such a market to make a profit from it.

Day Trading Options

Most traders are aware of day trading stocks but have little information about using the same strategy for options. As you may know, options traders make money buying and selling puts and calls. Although options offer high leverage that looks more wonderful when used in day trading, day trading options is often associated with several challenges.

The number one challenge is that of the premium value, which seems to reduce the fluctuation of prices on a daily basis. The options market is also faced with a lot of liquidity challenges, thus reducing the amount of profit one can make from day trading. This means that if you choose options as your day trading instrument, you will need to deal with the following two issues:

- Loss of capital

- Price and market movement

Despite these downsides, it does make sense to apply day trading strategies on options. This is made more possible for traders with smaller accounts since the risk of losing capital remains minimal. One main reason that can make you interested in this kind of venture is the low costs involved. Options always require less money to trade. Instead of purchasing shares only to sell them the same day, you may consider buying options and selling them after a few hours at a profit, however small.

Another advantage that options offer for day traders is the ease with which they can enter and exit the market. When trading options, you can quickly get in and out of the market, then when trading bonds, stocks, and mutual funds. Options contract always give the trader a chance to opt out when the market is not too favorable. This means that you can use this strategy to minimize the risk of losing your capital significantly.

Just like stocks, you must be able to identify the right kind of options for day trading. One standard method used to do this is technical analysis. The technique enables you to predict stock price movements which in return assist you in determining whether or not to invest in a particular stock's options.

When day trading options, you must choose those options that feature less time value. These are options such as the near month in the money because they possess very little time value, thus offering you the best opportunity to make money. If you pick an option that has a high time value, you will make very little profit from it. The reason why low time valued options provide more profit potential is because most people often trade them. Their prices are also bound to change significantly within a single day. They also feature narrower bid-ask spreads.

Day trading options requires a lot of training and practice. If you try to figure out the business on your own, you may make regrettable mistakes along the way that can cost your entire capital. The more you practice, the more confident you will become. It is also essential that you get the right options trading systems that support day trading. A good system will reduce your responsibility of analyzing the market by giving you the necessary market data for your daily trading activities.

To avoid losing so much capital in options trading, you can engage the use of limit orders. The profit made from day trading options is often derived from the difference between the ask price and the bid price. This can be as low as 2% of the price of the option. One thing that makes options day trading more complicated is the pricing model. The cost of an option depends on several factors. This means that the price of an option can deflate or inflate more rapidly than other financial instruments. If you are not quick enough to identify and take advantage of these price movements, you may not realize any profits.

Chapter 5: Day Trading Strategies

Day trading aims to close the day with profit generated from small price movements in financial instruments. Most people view day trading a very complicated trading strategy because it needs quick action for one to make a profit. This is why it is crucial to understand the several strategies used by traders to succeed in the trade.

Day trading strategies are different from other long-term strategies. They work to ensure that you make a profit from short trading periods. Day trading strategies comprise of rules and regulations that enable you to open and close positions successfully. Due to the large number of strategies available on the market today, it is important to understand the features you need to look for when selecting a strategy for your trading endeavors. Here are some few features you should check out for:

Accurate trading signals – a good strategy is one that has clear indications of when to enter or exit positions. These indications should be technically based. The easier it is to use your approach, the better time you will get to make trading decisions. This also applies to stop-loss rules. The strategy you choose should allow you to implement stop-loss techniques of your choice.

High rate of success – the success rate of your strategy should surpass the risk involved using the strategy. When using the strategy, you should be assured of more favorable returns. If you select a strategy with an 80% success potential, it means that 8 out of 10 trades will end in profit. The lower the potential for success, the higher the risk of loss.

The main goal for you as a day trader is to understand daily market trends and trade at the right time. Here is a glimpse into some of the common strategies used in day trading:

- *Momentum trading*

The strategy is utilized by day traders who employ technical analysis and not fundamental analysis for market analysis. Fundamental analysis is used to analyze stock based on some underlying factors such as the business earnings and debt value. Technical analysis, on the other hand, concentrates on changes in stock attributes such as the price and chart patterns. These attributes are often generated from the stock's price performance history.

The strategy is used by day traders when the price of stock assumes a relatively high or low price than average. These prices can be determined on hourly, minute, or half-hour intervals. Traders use these new prices as an opportunity to maximize profits from highly bullish or bearish markets. Although the strategy applies to any high and low points, most traders wait to use it on extremely high or low positions since this is where the profit is at peak.

There are several things the trader should look for when employing this kind of strategy in stock trading. These are:

- An extraordinary change in the price of the stock. This can be caused by an increase in the underlying company's earnings or financial news that impacts the stock in question.

- Stock price changes that go beyond 40 percent

- Smaller stocks that are bought or sold too quickly

- Ideas, trends or news that impact momentum trading

- *Breakout Strategy*

Can use this strategy when anticipating that the cost of a stock will rise beyond the highest resistance price experienced previously. This strategy works better with high volume trades. The breakout point for high volume trades always raises more profit than one for stocks with lower volumes. Mostly, stock prices begin to decrease as soon as they hit the resistance price until a factor arises on the market that can make the prices to rise again. This is because after the resistance levels; there are always more sellers than buyers on the market.

- *Scalping*

It's another day trading strategy used when one wants to sell off shares as soon as he buys them. This strategy is for you if you intend to engage in numerous trades each day for quantity and not quality. The goal of using this strategy is to accumulate small amounts of profits from each of these trades. At the end of the day, you end up with a large sum of profit.

Who use this strategy often looks out for trades whose price movement is less than 1 percent. They then enter the market and exit quickly, making some small profit from it. The strategy is quite defensive since it protects you from losing your capital. Most traders also use stop orders together with this strategy to minimize losses as soon as the market prices begin to deflate. For this strategy to work for you, you need to remain consistent in your trades. If you engage in very few trades per day, you may not be able to realize the kind of profit you are seeking to make.

You need access to real-time market and price information for the strategy to be efficient. This information will assist you to capitalize on every slight movement in stock prices. You can set a target price for the day and use the strategy to reach these target levels.

- *Pullback Strategy*

The strategy is always applied to stocks that have a specific price pattern. Traders are required to monitor this trend until it comes to an end then make trades as the prices begin to change. If the price was consistently going upwards, the entry point is where the price starts to decline. This point is referred to as the pullback.

Using this strategy, the trader employs the use of technical charts to determine the market trend.

Keen interest is often put on an uptrend that assumes several high prices. This movement indicates a looming decline in the price. When looking to short stock, you should check out for at least two consecutive decreases in the price. As soon as the price begins to rise, you take this as the pullback point where you enter your trades. Even if the price reverses after you have entered the market, you do not need to get worried. The trend can go on for a long time allowing you to make the best profits.

- *News Trading strategy*

Stock prices are often affected by financial news and other finance-related events. For example, when a company misses an earning, its stock cost may decrease significantly. This is why each day trader must begin the day by going through some critical news channels to determine if there's anything new in the business world.

News trading concentrates on the use of daily events and news. When there's bad news announced, you will need to sell your stocks in good time before the prices start to deflate. During this time, you might also want to buy the shares whose prices decline significantly for selling them at a profit. When the news is positive, you might want to purchase more stock before the prices start to rise. As the price increases, you can sell them at a good profit as well.

Options Trading Lingo

When learning about day trading options, there are several terminologies that you will come across. Understanding these terms helps you to trade effectively. Let us look at some options trading lingo that is basic for every trader.

- The strike price refers to the amount of money set as the cost of a specific option. When purchasing an option, the strike price refers to the value at which you buy the stock. When selling an option, the strike price is the amount you pay to acquire an option position.

- Exercise cost – this is the amount paid to the seller when you exercise or close an options position. Exercising an option means closing the contract associated with the option. Most day traders exercise options when the current price of the underlying security is more than the strike price set at the beginning of the trade. Since options have an expiration date, it is not a must that you exercise your options manually. However, you can do this if you are sure that by closing the position at the current point, you will gain some income from the trade. You may also decide to exercise positions when there is a looming risk of losing your capital.

- Expiration – each option has a date of expiration. This refers to the point when an option ceases to exist. You cannot trade an option position after it expires. At the end of the trade period, you either end up making a profit or a loss depending on your trading plan and market trends.

- Naked option – this is an option that does not give you ownership of the underlying stock. By now, you may have understood that options are only derivatives of other financial instruments. Trading in options does not necessarily allow you to own the underlying instrument. To make a profit from a naked call, you need to purchase an option at a lower price, wait for it to increase then sell the option. The difference between the closing price and the bid price becomes your profit.

- Premium – this is the amount of money you invest in a trade as a capital before you start trading.

- Underlying security – this refers to the financial instrument upon which an option is derived.

- Stop order – a stop order is a kind of order the trader uses to limit the price of an option from rising or declining beyond a certain point. The stop order is normally created below the current stock price and the position closes as soon as an option reaches this price.

- Contingent order – this order is only found in options trading. It is used to determine the trading process based on the value of the underlying security. Traders use this order when they want to exercise an option after the price of the underlying stock reaches a certain amount. These orders are therefore based on the stock price and not on the price of the option.

Types of Options

Put and call options are the basic types of options. Put options grant you the opportunity to sell a particular security to someone at a pre-agreed price. Call options, on the other hand, allow you to purchase stock from a trader at a preset price.

There are other types of options that are defined using different kinds of parameters. For instance, there are American style and European style options. American style options can be exercised before their day of expiration. This feature makes the options more flexible than European style options which can only be exercised on the day of expiration. You are therefore not allowed to exercise European options any time before this date is reached.

Another parameter used to define options is the mode of trading. There are exchange-traded options and over the counter options. Exchange-traded options are the most popular. They refer to those options transacted over an online trading platform through a broker. Options that are traded over the counter or OTC options as they are commonly referred to are not popular because they are not freely available to the general public.

Options can also be grouped in terms of the underlying security. For instance, stock options are those options whose underlying instrument is the shares of a particular company's stock. Index options are those whose underlying security is an index while futures options are those whose security is a futures contract. There are also basket options which utilize more than one instrument as the underlying security.

One more categorization of options is by their time of expiration. For example, regular options are those whose expiration cycle is quite standardized. These have set some months within the year cycle as expiration dates. Weekly options are those that expire after one week. These are quite unpopular since they are derived from a few numbers of financial instruments. Quarterlies expire after three months then LEAPS or long term expiration anticipation securities are options that feature prolonged contract durations. These options are top-rated because they are derived from a wide array of underlying instruments.

Other types of options include employee options, cash-settled options, as well as exotic options. With exotic options, the trading terms of the contract are always customized to suit buyer and seller preferences. Some examples of such options are binary options, barrier options, and compound options whose underlying financial instrument is another option.

How to Succeed in Day Trading Options

Becoming a professional day trader requires a lot of skill and planning. You must get into the market, knowing exactly how to generate income from the available opportunities. The level of volatility of many options prices makes it possible for you to gain some good cash from day trading them. However, when not handled cautiously, this volatility can lead you into a huge financial mess.

The primary determinant of success when day trading options lies in having a great plan. Each plan that you develop must be characterized by effective trading strategies. We already discussed some of the attributes you should consider when choosing a trading strategy. You must ensure that your trading plan remains simple enough. This will ensure that you do not engage in sophisticated processes that are difficult to understand and implement.

Here are some more tips you need to apply to ensure success when day trading options. Of course, you cannot become a millionaire day trader overnight. You need to exercise some patience as you implement these tips until you attain your trading goals.

1. *Invest in high potential opportunities*

Possess a high potential for significant profits. However, you must consider the risk involved in their volatile nature. When you target trades that possess a high profit potential, you must also understand the level of risk associated with such trades. Before entering any trade, make sure you know the cost implications should the market direction change against your expectations.

Of the hidden costs of options trading revolve around the time value. Options always cost less as the expiration date approaches. They undergo a process known as time decay. This implies that the longer you hold on an options contract before trading it, the more its value decreases. Trading an option in the morning is different from trading the same option later in the evening. You must always have a time expectation when day trading options. One way that you can minimize the effects of time decay is by trading options as soon as you can. You need to identify a strategy that allows you to do this. Options are associated with high returns and high risks as well. Before entering any position, assess the risks involved and know how to minimize them.

2. *Trade closer to the current price*

Always cost less when there is a considerable difference between their strike price and the price of the underlying stock. As a day trader, your intention is to make the most from each trade you engage in. To maximize your returns from options, stick to those whose strike price is close to the stock price. This is where most traders put their focus. Therefore it will be easy for you to make purchases, and sell those contracts you want to close.

3. *Have an exit strategy*

The serious mistake you can make as a day trader is engaging in options trading without a sound exit plan. As you control your emotions, make sure you understand when to exit a position before it gets too late. Plan your work schedules, define the amount of money you are willing to risk in the trade, and ensure that you do not deviate from these figures.

An exit plan is required at all cost. It doesn't matter whether the trade is going in your favor or against you. Set exit points for the upside and downside of the market way in advance. Besides these points, you also need to have clear timeframes for each trade so that you do not leave positions open for more extended periods than is necessary.

4. *Remain Disciplined*

Not let the market determine the course of your trades. Have some limits defined way before you begin trading. Doing this will save you from engaging in emotional trades. Set stop orders in good time to ensure that you limit any losses in case the market spread widens.

5. *Allow put and call strategies determine the course*

Options feature a different strike price. When choosing a contract to trade, choose the best in terms of the strike price. Enter call positions and allow these to meet the expectations of your market on the upside. Do the opposite for put options.

6. *Do not compound*

Interest is listed among the wonders of the world. This may be true. However, it is essential to understand where to use it in financial trading. You can easily engage this concept in stock trading. But it is not advisable to apply it when day trading options. Losing an entire capital is not something new in day trading, especially when trading options.

Not reinvest your profits whatsoever; unless you are sure that this move is going to earn you more profit. What you should focus on is how to leverage profits from the capital you have already invested. Keep preserving the profits to minimize your loss potential. Day trading options presents an environment that is full of risks. Leaving your profits to compound makes the deal even riskier.

Each tip that you apply in your options trades always keeps the time decay aspect in mind. If a position is approaching expiration and you have not reached your target, you can choose to end it before you lose more than expected. Have a plan for each kind of strategy you wish to implement. Do not focus on the profit alone, and do not allow any form of greed or emotion to drive you. Beware of exiting positions too early, as this can leave you with no profit at the end of the day.

Chapter 6: Day Trading Strategies for Beginners

Day trading is often characterized by sudden changes in price movements. This is why you need aggressive strategies to survive in the trade. There are strategies that will enable you to generate huge profits while others will only allow you to get some little returns.

As a beginner, you need to understand how the market behaves to succeed in your trading endeavors. The ultimate goal is always to make profit as you reduce the risks involved in each trade. You need a lot of patience and discipline to fully understand and apply some trading principles to your day to day activities. Here are some of the strategies you need to employ before and during the trading sessions to ensure that you succeed in the trade.

1. *Build a watch list*

   The stock market is made of several day trading opportunities that you can take advantage of. However, most traders miss out on a good number of these opportunities simply because they do not have any watch lists defined. To come up with an effective watch list, you first need to identify the kind of stock that supports the kind of strategies you wish to implement. Before you can achieve this, you must first acquire the necessary skills required for your trade.

It is easy to come up with a great watch list if you understand how the day trading market operates. You, for instance, need to understand how stock prices are determined and how economic cycles impact these prices. Another thing you need to define for you to create an effective watch list is the amount of time you are ready to spend on the trading platform. If you intend to spend only a few hours on the platform each week or month, you can create a list that has very few issues to follow up. If you intend to trade on a daily basis then you need to create a database with hundreds of issues that you need to track. You can always display items in your list on your screens as you trade as these will serve as a guideline for your transactions.

There are various aspects you need to consider if you want to build a strong watch list. Some of these include:

- *The account size.* With a small account size, you only need a few items on your watch list. The opposite is true for traders with large accounts. When trading, you can always scan through the list and select two or three items that you can execute concurrently. You can sort the items according to priority and choose those that allow you to diversify in terms of stock types and industry sectors. For instance, you may decide to trade in individual stocks as well as ETFs at the same time.

- *Time available.* You need to understand the amount of time you have available for trading. If you do not have enough time to track hundreds of items then concentrate on a small number that you can execute effectively.

- *Expertise in trading options.* This will determine whether you should include options in your watch list or leave them out entirely. In case you have the right knowledge to trade options, you can expand your watch list to include other types and strategies of trading instead of confining yourself on stocks. Such items include things like spreads and as well as other call/ put strategies. Since option strategies are always versatile with most market environments, it will be advantageous to you as you may end up making more profit than people who are focusing on stock trading alone.

As you consider these aspects, you must also concentrate on knowing what is on the watch list. You must learn how to track items like the duration of each trade and the volatility level just to understand the kind of risk involved. Master the attributes of each list item as you decide which one to prioritize. Ensure that you note any changes taking place on your list. This is most important when you are engaged in options trading.

2. Identify the right stocks

Not all financial instruments are ideal for day trading. You need to come up with a list of stocks you wish to trade in. These should be identified based on your trading needs and goals. Remember, not all stocks are the same, and not all can be traded using your preferred strategies. Therefore it is important that you keenly identify those stocks that can bring you more profit.

To do this, first you need to estimate the amount of capital you want to invest in the business. Once you have done this, you can research the right markets and settle on those that offer the right environment for you to trade. Each day in the time of a day trader brings itself new trading stocks and opportunities. You can always prioritize on the stocks that feature breakouts or those that are highly volatile. Such stocks offer better profit potential. Even stocks with average but consistent volatility are good for trading since you can always get something from them.

As a beginner however, you must confine yourself to a limited number of stocks each day. If you diversify too fast you may risk the little capital you have. There are several factors you need to consider when selecting the kind of stock to trade. Here are some of them:

- *Volume* – stock volume allows you to create positions depending on demand. When a stock features high volumes, it is easier to open and close positions associated to it. If it has low volume then you will struggle to buy or sell stocks and the day may end without you making good profits. The goal of creating orders is to ensure that they get filled at the right prices. Low volume stocks deny you this opportunity since the value of your order may be higher than the available number of stock shares at the time of trade.

- *Volatility* – when selecting stocks to trade in you must consider the volatility level. You therefore need to choose those with higher price movements during the day. Every stock always features a different percentage of volatility. Some stocks experience very small price changes while others always feature significantly large changes.

When checking volatility, have your trading style in mind. You also need to consider the kind of broker you have. For instance, there are traders who find it hard trading stocks that make large price changes. Such traders always concentrate on the stocks that move slightly per day. Stocks whose prices change too fast always need quick action during execution. If as a beginner, you have not mastered this skill, you may wish to avoid such stocks until you are confident enough to carry out such trades. You may need to invest in a stock screener to help reduce the stocks to a number that is manageable. You can specify the percentage of volatility you need and focus on these.

- *Price range* – this is another factor that you need to consider when getting the right stocks for your trade. You can either become a trend trader, range trader or both.

  With your stock screener, you can easily identify the kind of stocks that suit your mode of trading. In case you wish to focus on range trading, you should concentrate on those stocks that are likely to range. If you want to trend trade then you should select stocks that a tendency to trend. A good stock screener helps you to separate between trend and range stocks faster. If you decide to sort stocks manually, it may take you a long while and this means that you will miss out on some lucrative opportunities.

These three elements must be considered at the same time. If you fail to consider any of them, you may end up choosing the wrong type of stock to trade. A stock screener allows you to specify those parameters you wish your ideal stocks to have. The screener uses these parameters to list matching opportunities available on the market.

3. *Have entry and exit strategies in place*

As you begin trading, you may keep getting some excellent deals but if you do not understand when to enter or leave the market, day trading may not work for you. The amount of profit you gain from a trade depends on the kind of strategies you lay. Entry and exit strategies are quite numerous on the stock market. If you get the right ones and stick to your trading guidelines, you are most likely to succeed in day trading.

The following are some guidelines that you can use to ensure that your entry and exit strategies remain active throughout the trading session.

- Focus on the current trend. The stock market always experiences changes all the time. It is upon you as the trader to adjust your entry and exit strategies accordingly. For instance, when the market assumes an upward trend, you can trade long positions successfully and when it assumes a downward trend you can concentrate on trading short positions. Day trading trends do not last. You need to seize every opportunity as it comes and avoid postponing any opportunities.

Identifying certain trends requires a lot of skill and attention. Use trendlines to determine entry and exit points for your positions. You can come up with these lines in real time as the market changes. More trendlines often provide you with more alternatives in terms of the signals available for your transactions.

- When the market is rising, choose strong stocks. When it is declining, trade weak stocks. It is often rewarding trading stocks or equities that have a high correlation with indexes. Stocks that are weak when compared with indexes do not offer the best opportunities. Strong stocks always feature higher volatilities than weak ones.

This implies that you should seek to purchase stocks whose price is increasing faster than indexes and futures. When the price of the index and future start to decline, the value of stock will not drop that much, giving you a higher potential for profit. When the price of futures and indexes start to decrease, focus on selling stocks whose price is reducing faster than the futures. As the price of the futures changes in the downtrend, the cost of stocks may not change that much, resulting in higher profits as well.

- Work with pullbacks. Trendlines only give you a visual glimpse into the market and how the prices are set to change. It is upon you, therefore, to identify entry and exit points in such circumstances. One way to do this is through the use of pullback points.

The point when the price of a stock starts to move either upwards or downwards then suddenly changes direction is what is called a pullback. You need to start your trades at this point to facilitate maximum returns. The pullback acts as a signal to indicate whether you need to make an entry or exit on the market. You must be quite observant to be able to identify these points.

- Focus on making profits regularly. As you start day trading, you want to ensure maximum returns at the end of the day. Due to the dynamics of the market, you will always have some limited opportunities to make profit. Therefore, you do not have to spend a lot of time on trades that are not quite promising. Anytime a trade assumes the wrong direction, you can exit the market when it is still early enough to capture some small profits from the trade. You can do this by:

- o Taking the profits realized from a long position so long as the price is slightly higher than the former high in an uptrend

- o Taking profits in a short position when the price is lower than the former low price in the present trend

You can always mark entry and exit points on your day trading charts to ensure that you do not bypass them.

- Avoid trading in stagnant environments. Sometimes the stock market may stall. Prices do change most of the time, but not always. If the price is moving in small percentages, ensure that the change is large enough to give you more profit than risks before entering a trade. If the price is not trending but moving within a certain range, you may decide to engage in range trading instead of using the trend trading method. During this time, the price may keep moving up and down creating some resistance areas. Take not of these resistance areas to understand when to short sell or long buy positions.

When you are intending to purchase stock in this scenario, locate an exit point at the near top of the price range. If you want to sell, identify an exit point on the lower part of the range that is closer to the bottom. These two points present less risk and high reward. You may decide to create stop loss orders within the range to minimize any kinds of losses you may incur.

It is very easy for you to alternate range trading and trend trading within the same platform. You therefore need to understand how these trading methods work and what time to apply them. Expert traders often begin trading as soon as they get to the market. However, as a beginner, it is important that you take a few minutes each morning to understand how prices are changing and how certain stocks are performing before you start trading. This will help you identify those stocks that are volatile and those that are not. Professional traders always enter and exit positions fast because they have already identified the right trading strategies and discipline required.

4. *Spend quality time on the market.*

You may be wondering the right time frames to engage in day trading. This is a common concern for most beginners and you should not get worried about it. In order to understand the kind of market you are trading in and the patterns involved, you should always spend adequate time on the trading platform. You will be busy monitoring charts, identifying resistance and support levels and checking out price predictions. The kind of chart you decide to use affects the trading time-frame. For instance, you can decide to make use of one-minute trading charts when dealing with positions that need to be opened and closed quickly. However, you must understand that chart periods do not indicate how volatile a particular stock is. For instance, the one minute and five minute charts may both apply to stocks that have the same volatility at the same time.

As a day trader that is just getting started, you must beware of certain timeframes and monitor these closely. Before choosing a timeframe, you must understand that these offer relatively the same information, only the way the information is represented differs. In most cases, short time frames always possess more details than longer ones. Since most transactions take place as soon as the market opens in the morning, you need to use charts to monitor this time specifically. At this point is when most traders make large profits, others losses.

You may identify certain charts and use them the entire day to determine the right time frames to trade. Tick charts are the most used because they always offer traders with more detailed information. They also give you the opportunity to establish whether the market is moving or not. Individuals who focus on one minute and five minute charts are those who wish to monitor every kind of activity taking place on the market.

As hours go by, the chart you would have chosen will keep accumulating some bars especially if you are trading stocks that are largely volatile. Keep monitoring every trend, support and resistance levels as well as the volatility of stocks. Most day traders begin in the morning and by 11:30 they are done transacting. Those who continue with trading always keep of platforms over lunch hour since this period is often characterized by very little activity. Some proceed with the business in the afternoon whole others wait until the day is almost ending to start trading again. In the evening, most charts do not display activity for the entire day but only a few hours.

A good chart will also display price and market trends for prior days. Once you open such a chart, you will easily see this information and a lot more about the pre-market and what took place before the day began. However, you do not need to concentrate on past stock performances as a day trader since your focus should be on what is happening presently. You only need to focus on a stock's and market's history if the strategy you are using depends on it.

For a good number of day traders, stock charts always assist them when it comes to placing trades. The charts bear signals that indicate when the market is ideal for trade and when it is not. You must note that the cost of stocks may not be visible on your charts the entire day, yet you need this information to determine the overall performance of the market. You can use more than one chart at the same time to gain a better understanding of different time intervals. Doing this also improves your overall trading experience. The more you trade, the more you can increase your timeframes. Larger timeframes often provide you with a better view of the market. You may increase the number of hours, or customize these sessions to be able to see the price of stocks for the entire day. Once you master some chart patterns, you can comfortably work with shorter time frames and only use longer ones if your strategy requires that you do so.

5. Reflect on your trading experiences

Each trading day will always come to an end. This is the time that you need to evaluate how the day has been as a way of identifying what needs to change as you continue trading. You can also decide to step aside from your screens for a few days just to review your plans, strategies and guidelines. This is especially important if day trading has not been working in your favor.

Day to day reflections are very essential for each day trader. It helps you to refresh mentally as you prepare for the next day

6. *Check your trading frequency*

Most beginners get into the day trading with so much activity that they end up stuck in numerous positions that are not quite promising. It is advisable that as you get started, you trade less frequently until you gain a better understanding of the trading strategy and what it entails. While you are still seeking to adjust to what is happening on the market, it is better to trade less as this is one way of minimizing the risks you get exposed to. When you limit the frequency of your trades, you also get enough time to learn from each transaction that you make. Taking frequent breaks also ensures that you keep your emotions under control depending on the outcome of the previous trades. Here are some of the tips you need to focus on to ensure that you maintain a low trading frequency:

- Do not use scalping strategies

- Concentrate on charts that use larger time frames

- Do not enter or exit trades blindly. Only go for those that are promising in terms of the reward attached to them.

For the few trades that you engage in, ensure that you set stop loss orders for them. If possible, do not adjust these until the day ends. This is because most new day traders tend to make emotional decisions depending on their experience on the market. Often times, these decisions are not always effective and they lead to losses. For instance, you may start comparing the kind of losses and profits made within a day and when you realize that you have incurred losses. You may seek to adjust the current strategies to cover up for these losses. In the process, you may end up risking more of your capital and if the trade ends on the negative, you would have incurred double losses. You thus need to leave this attempt to professional traders who have mastered the use of objective analysis when making day trading decisions.

This also includes avoiding positions you do not have any skill or confidence over. If you know that you cannot control your emotions, it is important that you keep off environments and platforms that will expose you to them. Sometimes you may be required to note some activities down just to ensure that you keep your positions active for a period that is necessary. You can engage in both active and passive management of your positions. Passive management involves the use of day trading orders to set limits for each transaction. Active management is when you are involved in the entire trading process. It entails staying on the trading platform from the start of the trade until the end.

Passive management has one advantage over active management of your day trading transactions. It shields you from changing market parameters unnecessarily.

7. Learn to interpret trading patterns.

As earlier mentioned, day trading strategies operate using two categories of analysis – fundamental as well as technical analysis. When starting your day trading business, it is essential that you learn how to interpret the patterns resulting from these two methods of stock analysis. In case you wish to use technical analysis for your information needs, ensure that you use one that is chart-based. Have a single price pattern that you can apply to all your trades to ensure success. Chart patterns that appear similar over time indicate that a certain stock is likely to assume this same pattern over a longer period in future. You can analyze stocks historical patterns to identify such trends.

When seeking for day trading patterns, always check out for those that outline price actions that are both simple and easy to understand. In case you are unable to determine whether your chart has any patterns, it means that the kind of stock you are trading does not have one. This means that you will need to look for other ways to predict price movements for the said stock.

Getting the right market to trade in is always a plus for every day trade. Before you even get started, you must have already decided on the kind of market you wish to trade on. Every market has its own advantages and disadvantages. Some require more capital to trade than others. Always put this into consideration when thinking on how to get started. For instance, the amount of capital you need to day trade stocks is not the same as what you need to day trade futures. Each market also bears a different profit potential. This only points to one thing – the amount of capital you have when getting started. Once you identify a market, take your time to study its features. You cannot master all the aspects associated with it at once. Therefore you must exercise some level of patience when learning about it. Ensure that it is one you can afford before acquiring the necessary tools and equipment you need for the trade. With the right market and tools in place, you can then establish a time schedule that works for you. Get your strategies and keep practicing how to use them all the time. Choose those strategies that seem more effective over those that aren't. Use a demo account to do this since it just works like a real account. Prepare yourself for any losses, since these will occur once in a while. But ultimately, do not invest cash that you are not ready to lose.

Chapter 7: Day Trading Success

The success of your day trading business depends on a lot of things. If you start on the right foot, you will definitely earn good rewards. The number one secret lies in remaining disciplined and neutral in the sense that your decisions remain independent of your emotions. Doubt, fear and greed should be the last things on your mind. As a beginner, you must not allow day to day occurrences to affect you. Although emotional changes are common, they should not influence the way you carry out your trades.

See price movements as something you should adjust towards since these will never be the way you wish them to be. Even when the market assumes a direction that does not favor you, you should not lose focus. There are several attributes that define successful day traders. These are people who:

- Are ready to risk their money in the trade

- Manage money in a great way

- Have confidence in the outcome of each trade

- Are not afraid to enter and exit positions

- Are disciplined and patient in their trading

- Customize very few strategies that work in their favor

Common Day Trading Mistakes and How to Avoid Them

The stock market is one of the best day trading environments because it has very few regulations for new traders. As long as you have a stable internet connection, a computer and some little cash, you can freely join other day traders. However, doing this does not assure you of profits. Quite a number of things need to be accomplished before you can celebrate success. Before you engage in the trade, here are some of the mistakes you need to beware of and to avoid.

1. Adding more capital to a trade that is going down – new traders always get tempted to average positions down when the price is on the decline with the hope that things will get better. This is one of the worst mistakes that you can do. The market prices may decline further resulting in exponential loss. Instead of doing this, set stop orders early into the trade and close positions as soon as things become bad.

2. Continuing to trade even after losing consecutively – when day trading, there are two figures you always need to have at the back of your mind. The risk/ reward rate as well as the win rate. The win rate is often represented as a percentage. For instance if you win 30 out of 50 trades, your rate of winning is 60%. Successful traders are those who are able to maintain at least 50% or more as the win rate. The risk/ reward ratio refers to the amount you win as compared to the amount you lose in each trade. For instance if your winning trades cost $80 and the losing trades are $40 then the reward/ risk ratio becomes $80/$40 which is 2. To be considered successful, this ratio should always be at least 1

3. Not setting stop loss parameters – not setting stop loss orders in your trade will always lead to danger. The work of stop loss orders is to limit the amount of capital you lose when market prices deflate against you. They moderate losses on your behalf

4. Working with the wrong broker. Trusting a broker with your capital is one of the best ways you can grow your day trading business. However, if you choose a broker that does not understand how to manage your cash you will end up losing most of

your fortune. You also need to understand how much commission the broker will charge in advance and if there are any hidden charges associated with the partnership. Beware of scammers who also parade themselves as brokers. These can lure you into investing in non-existent platforms.

5. Taking several related trades. As you start day trading, you may get excited at the many opportunities available on the trading platforms. This can lead you into opening multiple positions at the same time. You may end up getting these positions from the same stocks and this can become risky if the particular stock does not perform well on the market. When day trading, diversification is key. It protects you from losing too much on one type of stock. However, as a new trader, you need to be watchful of the number of trades you open in a day. You may be tempted to make multiple trades as way of minimizing the risk of loss. But this is not a good idea if you are not quite conversant with the market.

6. Investing what you are not ready to lose – if you are not comfortable losing the amount of cash you are investing into day trading, simply do not do it. Most

day traders get into the business without defining how much they are ready to lose. After they have lost the cash, they get frustrated. You should only risk 1 percent of your capital on each trade by setting your stop loss orders correctly. When you do this, only a small percentage of your cash will be lost at the end of the day, however much you trade.

As much as you would have set your loss limits, it is essential that you try to manage any ongoing losses and maintain them at a minimum low. If you keep losing at most 1 percent on each trade, you would have to part with a huge percentage of your capital at the end of each trading period. The fact that you have defined the loss limits does not necessarily mean that you have to lose this amount.

7. Entering the trade blindly – there are new traders who ignore their strategies completely, getting into the trade with no particular plan. This occurs partly when an individual keeps gaining on several trades in a row. When this happens, you can become overconfident that you cannot lose a trade. This confidence can make you invest everything you have, and this can lead to tremendous losses.

8. Not carrying out an analysis of the market. Once you have made a number of successful trades, you may start trading without analyzing the necessary market and financial data. It gets dangerous when you get into the market without understanding how the prices will change in future. Although long-term fundamental analysis is unnecessary for day traders, you need to understand this information for your future trades.

9. Not having a plan. This is one of the biggest mistakes day traders do. A trading plan often outlines the strategies and activities you need to engage in during the trade. It handles the when and how parts of day trading. When you do not have a plan, you may keep entering and exiting positions without any guidelines. Doing this will leave you unsure of what to expect from the trading period. Not having a plan also means that you are unable to estimate the risks involved in each trade you engage in.

10. Predicting news before it comes out. Some traders get to know of upcoming news and act on it even before it is released to the public. This looks like staying ahead of the market but it actually is not. It

is not advisable that you take positions before any news item gets confirmed. The stock price may move in either direction and this direction may change too fast. You need to understand this and trade basing on the current market trend, not unconfirmed news.

Day Trading Tips and Advice

As you begin day trading, there are several methods you can use to ensure you increase your chances of making profit. Some of these include the inside bar strategy, gapping up and down as well as the use of Fibonacci patterns.

1. *The inside bar breakout strategy*

    This is a strategy that utilizes two bars to assist you in day trading. One bar is always smaller than the other. The first bar is known as the mother bar while the other bar is the inside bar. The bar is used in day trading to identify the trend's direction. When you trade this way, the process is called breakout playing. The intention is always to place stop orders for buying or selling either at the top or bottom of the mother bar. These orders are then filled when the price goes beyond the bar edges. If the mother bar is relatively large, the stop orders can be placed at the middle of the bar.

2. *Gapping up and gapping down*

Gaps refer to price breaks often displayed in stock charts. These gaps always occur when there is a sudden release in a news item that impacts the price of stocks. The announcement may be about a new product release, mergers and acquisition or wars. These are always influential enough on the price of stocks. Gaps are always represented on the charts as a blank space between bars.

Gaps offer great signals that help you determine whether to purchase or you're your trades. When there is a gap down, this is the right time to sell your positions. When there is a gap up, it is the right time to purchase stock. When a price gap occurs, you may spend a few minutes studying the market range before you can decide what to do with your positions.

Generally, there are four primary gap types.

- o Full gap up – this is a gap created when the day's opening price for a certain stock is higher than the highest price attained by a stock the previous day

- Partial gap up – this is when the current opening price is below the stocks lowest price for the previous day

- Full gap down – this is created when the day's opening price is lower than the lowest price attained by a stock the previous day

- Partial gap down – this is when the current opening price is lower than the previous day's closing price but higher than the day's lowest price

Besides sudden news items, gaps can also result from certain technical and fundamental factors. For instance, if the earnings received by a certain organization are more than the anticipated amount, the price of the stocks related to the company may change drastically by the following day. This implies that the opening cost will be much higher than the previous day's closing amount.

Gaps can also be categorized by the position where they occur. For example, a gap located at the end one pattern and at the beginning of a new pattern is known as a breakaway gap. One that is located close to the end of a trend is an exhaustion gap. A common gap takes place outside the price pattern while a continuation gap is always at the center of a pattern or trend.

3. *Afternoon breakout strategy*

Although most day traders spend their morning hours on the market, there is always a higher possibility of making money from breakouts in the afternoon. Trading breakouts during morning hours is always easy because of the large volumes associated with the time period. Doing this in the afternoon requires a lot of skill because the stock is less volatile. The target of this strategy is to trade in stocks whose high and low prices reached the previous day have not been exceeded.

You can use this strategy by placing some limit orders either below or above the highest and lowest prices attained for the day. As the prices start to break out, the limit orders get filled and this results in some good profit

4. *Fibonacci retracement pattern*

These patterns are used to indicate trading points where the prices moving against a certain trend change to assume the right direction. The patterns work using the Italian number series that have been in use since the 13th century. The next number in the sequence is derived by adding the two previous numbers.

Fibonacci patterns are always applied in highly trending stock prices. The trader uses this strategy with the hope that when the price assumes a pullback, the amount will be equal to one of the numbers in the Fibonacci sequence. Most people use this technique to determine turning points for the market. However the points indicated by the patterns are only estimates and sometimes not accurate. There is only a certain level of possibility that the stock price will turn at the indicated points. The strategy is more effective when the prices are changing drastically. If you use it on slight price changes, you may not get any meaningful results.

The Psychology of Day Trading

Day trading involves a lot of emotions. This explains why you need to understand the place of psychology in trading. To become a successful day trader, it is essential that you develop a system that enables you to remain calm when trading to avoid overreacting to certain occurrences. Doing this requires a lot of effort and determination. You need to take control of your mind and be able to guide it towards achieving the success you need. This requires a lot of training. Below are some of the tips you can apply to improve your trading psychology.

1. *Have a clear mindset* – engage in exercises that motivate you as a trader. Keep reflecting on the attributes of the stock market and your ability to adjust to these attributes. Learn to appreciate yourself when you win, and to encourage yourself in case of a loss. Wake up early enough to plan your schedules ahead of the trading sessions. Get enough rest to ensure that your head stays clear during each trade.

2. *Engage in more practice* – when trading for the first time, you may lack the necessary confidence for the market. As you continue doing it, you may realize that the process is becoming simpler and easier. Your mental capability also increases as you continue trading.

3. *Diversify your knowledge* – keep learning about day trading. The more you understand about day trading the easier it gets for you when making some important trading decisions. Understand the basic as well as the technical skills required for day trading.

This will help you navigate through the risks associated with certain positions.

4. *Remain optimistic* – see yourself winning in each trade you start. This will help you set the right strategies. Visualize the market beforehand and motivate yourself to carry out each step required to succeed on the market. You can do this by highlighting the goals for the day and tuning your mind to achieve these goals.

As you do this, also remember to ready yourself for the worst. Prepare yourself psychologically for any shortcomings you may encounter along the period. Have a worst case scenario in mind and adjust your mind accordingly.

5. *Imitate successful day traders* – this does not mean that you copy everything that another trader is doing. It only means that you observe what others do differently and borrow that which might be of benefit to you. Note some positive attributes and behaviors. Incorporate some of these in your strategy or plan to ensure success.

As you continue to practice, monitor any changes or improvements over a period of time. You can do this by noting any daily occurrences in a journal. This can be handwritten or a document saved on your laptop. Whatever you note down will assist you to track any growth as you progress with your trading activities.

How to Control Your Emotions after Recording a Loss

The psychology of trading is quite delicate. Each time you register a win, you will always feel confident and excited. Any time you lose, you may feel frustrated and angered by the turn of events. In case you register a loss, do the following:

1. Do not change the initial plan – however tough the situation gets, stick to your initial plan. Most people tend to revise their day trading plan soon after registering a loss. This move always leads to more mistakes. Learn to stick to your plan at all times.

2. Revise your stop orders - check your stop orders to ensure that they are set at the right positions. These specify when you wish to buy and sell your positions. The amount you receive or issue out once a stop order is filled is known as the stop price. Doing this ensures that you put a limit to the direction your trades take. You can do this physically through your broker, but you may also set mental

stops. A mental stop is a decision you make to close positions before they get too risky. You physically exit the market once you realize that things are going against your anticipations.

3. Continue learning – remain focused and disciplined. Continue seeking the right information about day trading and apply these on the market. Study stock price movements, revise your actions and trading times and keep improving on your strategies.

Winning vs. Losing in Day Trading

Day trading is the fastest form of investment with instant returns. Although the strategy can be time consuming but very rewarding. A winning attitude always results in good profits.

Several factors always differentiate between winning and losing traders. Let us discuss some of them:

- Reduction of risk – day trading is a short term strategy encompassed with so many risks. Winning day traders often seek to minimize these risks as a way of maximizing their profits. They always look for the right training and information necessary for managing risks. They also do not limit themselves when it comes to learning new trading skills. Losing day traders on the other hand assume that the short-term trading technique does not require a lot of knowledge and experience. These end up making several serious mistakes. Such traders rarely have their accounts full because they keep losing their deposits. They rarely stay in the market for long; some always give up along the way.

- In case of loss, a losing day trader will start researching on new ideas and systems for trade. The trader will then attempt to implement these concepts on his subsequent transactions. The problem is that these concepts may be unverified and thus may make things worse for the trader. Winner on the other hand treats a loss with so much strategy. They always take time to analyze the loss, and then revise their plan according to their findings. Winners rarely get rid of their trading plans and systems, but losers keep replacing these more often.

- Losing day traders always concentrate on future trends. Winning traders concentrate on the current market trends and how to leverage these. As a trader, if you keep focus on the right trends, there is a high probability of success. It becomes difficult for you if you want to do a future analysis and trade at the same time. Day trading does not require a lot of analysis. It is better for a trader to track their risk than the profit potential.

- Some of the losers always copy everything done by other popular traders. For instance, they may translate an entire set of strategies used by most investors to their trading plan. This results in trading frustrations and more losing experiences. The successful day trader avoids mimicking what others are doing in entirety. They only pick what is useful and disregard what does not apply to their strategy.

- Losing traders find it hard to identify opportunities with high profit potential. This is because they get blinded with the general status of stock prices but do not dig deeper to understand how they can leverage such a status in their favor.

- Winning traders have a check on their emotions. They analyze the markets and trade without being mindful of how they feel. Losers always struggle with their emotions. They enter and exit positions based on how they feel. This results in illogical moves that cannot generate any income.

It is always easy for winning day traders to admit their mistakes and master any negative reactions arising from negative circumstances. These always identify any obstacles to their growth and work towards overcoming them. Losers always seek to justify their actions. They believe they are always right and take time to admit their mistakes. Even if they do not understand a market process, they will still seek to engage in the process without thinking about the consequences.

Most individuals who take day trading more seriously end up making very little from the trade. Experienced traders always find pleasure in everything they do. They are flexible to any changes in the market environment and do not take everything too serious.

Day trading Traps and How to Avoid Them

Stock trading entails a number of traps. As a person that engages in day trading, you want to be aware of these traps so that you can learn how you avoid them. Failure to do this can lead to an unpleasant experience and outcomes on the stock market.

By definition, a trap is any circumstance where the market assumes an unexpected direction contrary to the indicators you had received. In this case, you are always torn between following the market trend and sticking to the predictions made by technical indicators. A trap places you at a spot where you do not know whether to move with the market or against it. Some of the common traps are:

1. *Stock performance chart trap* – this occurs when it becomes difficult to understand whether a chart breakout is real or fake. It also occurs when you are not sure if a stock's price trend is really changing, or if it has just assumed a brief subtrend.

   If you are not careful in this case, you may interpret the charts wrongly and this will lead to unfavorable results. The trap can make you believe that you are trading in the direction of the market while you are not. You can eliminate this from your trading plan by automating the entire process. This will mean that you purchase software that will help you analyze the market more accurately as you locate the right opportunities to trade.

2. *Contrarian trap* – a good number of day traders always end the day registering a loss. Once you understand this, you may be tempted to do the opposite of what other traders are doing. However, the reason why traders lose a lot of capital is not

that they are doing things wrong. It may just be an issue with how they set up their limit orders and how they exit the market.

This trap occurs when you start trading against the current market trend. Since the market will be trending in the opposite direction, you will not be able to make any cash from your contrary transactions. To avoid this trap, ensure that you always stick to the current trend.

Overtrading and How to Prevent It

Overtrading simply means opening too many positions on the market at the same time. It is a psychological occurrence that a trader uses to minimize losses and maximize returns. This is never the case since most people that overtrade often struggle to manage their capital. Here are some steps you should take to prevent yourself from overtrading.

- *Taking a break after loss* – when you experience loss, do not be in a rush to lay strategies that will help you earn your money back. This can lead you into creating some unnecessary positions.

- *Have a limited number of setups* – if you wish to trade breakouts, have a limited number of trades you can transact in this setup.

- *Do not trade the whole day* – most day traders do not trade the entire day. You do not need to do this either. Once you attain your targets, you can spend your time doing other things.

- *Have loss and profit limits* - set these limits way before you start trading. once you achieve them, you can close business and resume the following day

- *Have a predefined number of stocks you wish to trade each* day - This may be challenging given the large number of stocks on the market today. However, you must limit yourself if you wish to avoid excessive trading.

Chapter 8: Money Management for Success

Money management mainly involves budgeting, saving, investing and spending ones money. Another way to explain it would be how an investor makes wise investment decisions with their funds and how they make plans around it. Making money is one thing, but knowing how to spend it wisely is what makes the whole difference. There are so many people who would be able to lead a great life, only if they managed their finances well. Unfortunately, this is not something that comes automatically, but rather something that needs a lot of discipline and prior preparation.

In the investment industry, money management is a wide topic that comes with solutions to wise investments. In the financial market, consumers always have access to wide range of investment opportunities, but depending on how they manage their funds, they might find themselves making wrong money moves. An investor's min goal is always to increase their net worth; hence they have to have great money management skills. Some would learn it themselves; while a few would always opt for financial advisors or money management apps, that then manages their money for them.

Simple Ways to Manage Money

1. Put down a budget

This applies to both small amounts of money or even any planning involving a lot of money. Budgeting helps a lot in having control over what or how one spends their money. Many people do not work with budgets as they think it is a useless process. However boring it is, budgeting gives you a clear picture of the amount of money you have and will help you limit yourself in spending on wrong things. Budgeting also helps one not to get into debts or live beyond their means.

A simple way to budgeting:

- Set realistic goals: Be it in investments, saving, etc., always set goals that you can achieve. Once you have goals to achieve, it becomes easier to work towards achieving them.

- Identify your expenses: Since most people know how much they make or have, they rarely bother to look into their expenses. Track down your expenses to the last coin for a certain period of time. It can be a few weeks or month.

- Identify your needs vs. your wants: Know what you need and what you want, as in this difference is where the problem lies. Knowing what you can live without will always make a huge difference as you get to set clear priorities for yourself when it comes to money matters.

- Create your budget: Working with the needs, write down a budget breakdown for yourself, making sure you are not spending more than you make.

2. Stick to the budget

Once you have the budget created, it only makes sense if you can stick to it to the latter. It would be a waste of time not working alongside the created budget, as it is the guide to spending. Refer to it along the way as you get things done, ensuring that you are not going beyond the amount allocated to the specific areas.

3. Have a limited miscellaneous fund

This is very critical when working with budgets, as it allows you some wiggle room to spend outside the budget. This is what one can use for fun or entertainment, but it has to be up to a certain limit. With the limit, one can be able to know how far they can go with the spending. Without a limit, the chances of spending too much on mere wants and not needs are very high.

4. Track your spending

Small frequent purchase always adds up quickly. This happens without ones knowledge, but before they know it, they have exhausted their finances. Tracking ones expenses gives one room to see where they are spending too much on any unnecessary purchases. Other people spend out of habit, even when they do not need the items. Tracking this sets a way of controlling how one gets to use their money on the most important needs.

5. Go for the best prices

When making purchases, always do a lot of comparison to go for the lowest and best prices. This can also be used in investment, where an investor with scout the market for affordable assets that are still great in value. Some items that are highly priced are because of mere differences in packaging, or branding. Always take advantage of discounts, coupons or clearance sales that always have prices lowered. This helps in saving money.

6. Do long term planning for big purchases

Once you have tracked the expenses are have started to make sense out of it, have a long term plan for any big purchases. This means one can start by saving and putting away fund even for investment. Rather than maybe taking a loan to invest, one can take a year to put away money for the same and they would not feel the heavy impact on their money.

Planning this in advance also helps an individual discipline themselves even more on where to spend and where to save.

7. Keep practicing

Once you have a clear picture of what works for you as an individual, keep practicing it to make it a habit. With time, you will be able to manage any amount of money and will know when to spend it or not. Even as an investor, you can be able to grow your portfolio by know when, when and how to invest.

How Much to Invest For Trading

Money management is a big deal when it comes to business investments. Also, knowing how, when and where to invest needs a lot of financial management knows how. In business, one must always know and be willing to take risks in order to grow their money. While it may be pretty simple, how one decides to go about this practice determines so much in the outcome.

There are successfully investors who planned and managed their funds and grew their way up to great success. This was done without taking on any loans. For this to be possible, one needs very high money management skills. On the other hand, these are those who thrive on sourcing for money or getting outside support for growth. This would also require good management skills as other people's money is involved.

For a business or investment to run well, there should be some simple money management procedures one can follow to be able to comfortably manage their funds:

1. *Estimate the startup cost*

   Come up with a detailed list of what would be needed as a start. The kind of supplies and equipment need for operating the investment or business. One way of doing this is to get financial advisors or working with people who have gone before you, to give you an idea of what is expected.

2. *Work on a working capital estimate*

   Before doing anything, figure out how much money you would need to keep the business or investment running. This is from utilities, salaries if any, rent, etc. Come up with a list of items that you would need to take care of in the near future. This is the time one can work with accountants or consultants who are more informed about such planning.

3. Have a six-month cushion

When setting up business operations, especially for a new company or investment, it is always advisable to have a six-month back up plan. This is because some businesses take a while to pick and be stable. Some can take even a year, which is why it is always said the first year in a business is the most crucial. When you have the cushion, one would not have to worry about sustaining it or lack of finances the first few months. This helps in buffing the operations until when they are stab=le.

4. Add any forgotten or foreseen fees

When running a business, there are times when one can forget some small but very important tasks, which should constantly be in the management plan. These are always a requirement for smooth operation, as they are mandatory fees in any kind of business.

- Tax:
- Minor utilities (phone, internet)
- Fuel expenses
- Other services and maintenance fees

Understanding Risk / ratio

Common risks to avoid in money management

There are so many ways one can avoid making money mistakes, but there are a few basic ideas on how to go about it. So many business owners and investors learn through their mistakes, but it does not always have to be the case for everyone. Here are a few examples on how to make great money decisions as a beginner:

Not working with a financial plan

When working with any kind of funds, and with no tangible financial plan, always ends up in a mess. This is one risk most people make and end up spending money haphazardly and without knowing it, have nothing to show for the spending. One always ends up going back to the drawing board once they realize they have incurred costs on so many things that they cannot account for. This is an area that needs a lot of caution be it for business men, households or even normal office set ups.

Not measuring and having an idea where your money goes

Not knowing how much one Is spending on a business or investment is very risky, as it leaves room for financial mistakes. Buying or having random expenses always leads to over spending and one might end up prioritizing wrong things. Always have a clear idea of what you need to spend on and have it written down, so you can stick to the plan to the latter. That way you can be able to track and see where you spend most of your money, and how to cut down on some of the costs.

Borrowing money that one does not need

There are people who borrow money just for the sake of borrowing, or just because they have access to the funds. This is a very dangerous move because one always ends up spending money on wants and not needs. As much as one has access to money, it is advisable to only borrow money when with a clear plan of how the money is going to be spending, and how much returns will come out of it.

Also, only borrow money when your plan. Is ripe, so that you do not end up having the money lying idle in your account hence tempting you to spend. Money always finds use whether one had plans for it or not.

Not budgeting for non-monthly expenses (holidays, lunches, vacations)

There are people who go for holidays without making any plans. They get into their investment fund; take a chunk of the money just to take a break. This is a very bad financial move as the funds should be put into great use in order to have high return on any investment. Holiday or vacations are good, but should be planned for in advance. This also helps in controlling the spending. Have a clear budget for the expenses, and then work out on a plan to achieve the budget, working with specific timelines.

Spending more than is needed

Impulse purchases are also a downfall to many when it comes to money management. When one spends too much or more than they are needed, it always becomes a habit and money gets wasted. This is most common in day to day expenses where one buys small things that will end up accumulating and make a great expense. Always spend money on things that are a need and not nice to haves.

Surviving on paycheck to paycheck

Majority of the society falls in this category of poor money management. They survive on one paycheck to the other and it would be disastrous if they lost their day jobs. Paychecks are great, but they are not the best when it comes to the high level of unemployment and company's cutting costs.

It is advisable to always have something on the side that one can use to boost they usual paycheck. This can be any kind of business whose money can be used for bigger investments. Also, with the paycheck, one still needs to use the money management tips shared to be sure they are utilizing it well to their growth and benefit.

Not having a plan around managing of one's monthly paycheck is risky, as it also makes one a slave to employer.

Saving after spending

The most efficient way to save money is never saving after budgeting for everything else, but rather saving first then plan for the remaining money. The mistakes people make is they do the reverse, and everyone knows how money issues are. One will always find a use for the money.

Expenses are always many in every setting of life, hence for one to be disciplined, they need to learn that saving is the most important aspect of budgeting, and that is should come first.

Not having emergency fund

An emergency fund refers to money that you set aside to use when you need something fast. If you find yourself struggling with every issue that comes up in the road, then you need an emergency fund. Working with an emergency fund is similar to operating a business without any savings at all. The emergency fund protects you from any unexpected expenses that might come your way. Let us look at the reasons why you need an emergency fund as a day trader:

- You have been trading and you have found yourself in debt. The emergency fund makes it possible for you to get out of debt and then cover anything that you might need to handle while running the business.
- You have just learnt about budgeting and you need to handle some expenses that come up. When you have an emergency fund, you will be able to add the expenses in the budget the way they come up. When you have an emergency fund, you can handle unexpected emergencies that come up in trading.
- If you are basing all your decisions and spending on just a single source of income, you need to

have an emergency fun. The fund will help you in the cases when your trades aren't going the right way and you need to have them working the right way.

- Since you are a trader, you are self-employed. This means that you will not have the chance to ask for unemployment benefits at all. Instead, you will need to have a good emergency fund that will help you handle all your expenses so that you live well while waiting for trades to go through. Remember as you place trades, you need to pay bills and do other things that will see you through the day.

Chapter 9: Brokers

Who Is A Broker?

This is someone who buys and sells goods or things on behalf of someone else. They mostly are middle men in transactions, that often they make profit out of. They only have to organize and plan for transactions to take place between a purchaser/buyer and a vendor/seller. The broker ends up getting a commission out of the deal, either from the buyer or seller. Most of the time they represent the seller.

Brokers may be individuals or firms. When it is a firm, it still acts as a go between their customer and the vendor.

Brokers exist in many different industries. An example would be real estate brokers who advertise and sell properties on behalf of the owners. We also have insurance brokers who sell insurance on behalf of firms. We have stock market brokers who work on the stock market.

Why Use A Broker?

There are a few advantages of using brokers In any kind of business. As usual, before getting into any business with a broker, always do intensive research on what you are about to get into. There are a few bad crops in the market.

1. *They know their market well*

   Most brokers are people or firms who have been in the field for quite a while and always know what is best for one client to the other. They also know who to talk to if you need anything specific and always do it well knowing they will benefit.

   Brokers have been on the market for a long time and have seen what goes on and know too well what to expect. They have all the information you need right from the time you enter the market to the time you leave. They are particularly important when you are entering a foreign market that you aren't familiar with. You need to take time and look for the perfect broker that will tell you what you need and how to do things the right way. However, you need to be wary of the brokers who are out to exploit you. Use referrals and other methods to try and get the right broker who understands your needs.

2. Wider representation

A client is able to reach more people or a wide marker when using a broker, compared to them doing it by themselves. Brokers are also quite affordable, and have a network they work with; hence there is limited cost incurrence with them. Because most of them are well known, they are able to reach a wider market ratio easily.

When you decide to work with a broker, you get to cast your net wider so that you can get better business. Coming up with a network takes time, which is why it is just right that you work with a person that already has a network which you can tap in. This saves you time and effort, as well as money. Take time to work with a broker that already has a network of established clients.

3. Special skills and knowledge

Brokers mostly have special knowledge of the field they are in and are good at the specific brokerage area. This is because they work in detail so as to know the needs of different types of clients. Because of this, they are an asset to anyone who is looking for their services.

The skills that a broker has vary from customer relationship management to money management. They will help you to grow your empire as you sit and wait for them to do the work you want. It takes experience and a lot of patience for you to learn the skills and be able to do the things that a broker can do. So, always make use of a broker when making trading decisions.

4. *Customer choice*

Brokers always work with the customer's choice. They will always want to know what one needs they will always endeavor to ensure the customer is satisfied and has what they originally wanted, or better.

5. *Time saving*

Because they mostly know their trade well, a broker would be able to achieve more within a shorter period of time for the customer. This is because of their great networking within their field of specialization. They always know where to find what, at what time and for what amount.

The time that you save when you work with a broker can be used to handle other tasks that you have. Take time to make sure the broker knows what they are doing otherwise you will end up wasting a lot of time.

Types of Brokers

- Stock broker
- Business broker
- Pawn Broker
- Information broker
- Insurance broker
- Investment broker

Roles Played By Brokers in Forex Trading

For a long while, people have been quite skeptical about the Forex market, but this is something that has been growing rapidly the last few years. Forex trading has become one of the leading markets in the trading world. It generally involves the process of changing one currency to another for certain reasons. Currencies trade against each other depending on the exchange rates and brokers use the growth on these rates to make profits.

Because of this, there has been a high need of Forex brokers who are the middle men for investors who want to invest in Forex. Forex brokers are usually people or firms that provide currency traders with a platform to buy and sell their currency. They end up controlling a small portion of the large Forex market.

Their importance varies from need basis:

1. *Link between the trader and the market*

   There are many investors who have a lot of funds and want to grow their wealth in Forex trading, but have no idea how to go about it. This is where brokers come in, and act as their representatives in the Forex market. Brokers know all the nooks and crooks of Forex trading, and always know when to take advantage of the exchange rate changes. They are best placed to give advice on how to go about trading, as they are always doing it as a day job hence very experienced.

   Brokers always know when to take advantage of the market and the different events that would lead to an increase or decrease in the exchange rate, and hence know when to make the right moves. This they do at a smaller fee, so their aim is to have as many clients as possible so they can thrive on numbers.

2. *Help educate investors or other beginner brokers*

   Brokers have lots of information on trading than most people would, and it is advisable for any beginner to have one to share tips with them. They would know how to go about avoiding some basic mistakes people make when they start investing in Forex markets.

3. *They trade and negotiate on behalf of investors*

   Brokers are mostly the same as sales representatives. They trade currencies online, and the skilled ones do it as a daily job hence very useful for any beginner investor.

   There are very many investors who want to trade but have no time, hence use brokers who do it full time. The Forex market is a 24 hour business operation and the exchange rates tend to rise and drop every moment. This means anyone trading has to always be on standby to make a move. Brokers do this on behalf of other people who have the money to invest but have no time.

   This as times is most ideal as the brokers always know the right moves that bring in profits and incase of losses, they always know the move to make to reduce the amount of losses made.

4. *Advise traders on risks that come with Forex trading*

Forex trading, just like any other trading in the stock market, is a risky affair. As it highly involves currency values, there are times that the fluctuations can affect the market and a broker should be keen enough to know the right move to make.

Every investment has pros and cons, which are risks that investors will encounter one way or the other. One might lose more than the value of their transaction, but with a skilled broker to guide you through, you might be able to salvage the situation.

Major risk factors one might encounter:

Exchange rate risk: this is the risk that comes by as a result of changes in the value of the currency. There is a constant shift on the worldwide supply and demand balance, which might end up affecting the traders' position. This mostly depends on whichever way the currencies will move based on different factors. It is in this case where a broker advises one to cut losses early enough by taking different positions. These could be the position limit or loss limit. Other risks include:

- Interest rate risk
- Credit risk
- Country risk
- Liquidity risk
- Transactional risk
- Risk of ruin

5. Customer support during local trading hours

6. Ideas on latest trading platforms

Before you can work with a broker, you need to choose one. Choosing a broker isn't an easy task at all because you have hundreds of brokers to choose from. The best thing to do in this case is to try and make sure you work with referrals and testimonials when making a decision. Base on facts when getting the right broker.